11/96

Kevin & Sue

"Hold

To your Dreams

Carol H Gadra

MW01241342

The White Porcupine

The White Porcupine

Carol J. Howard

VANTAGE PRESS
New York

FIRST EDITION

All rights reserved, including the right of
reproduction in whole or in part in any form.

Copyright © 1996 by Carol J. Howard

Published by Vantage Press, Inc.
516 West 34th Street, New York, New York 10001

Manufactured in the United States of America
ISBN: 0-533-11912-x

0 9 8 7 6 5 4 3 2 1

To Mark Watson and Ken Day, without whom there
would be no reason

Fear ye not therefore, ye are of more value than many sparrows.

—*Matthew 10:31*

Contents

The White Porcupine

The White Porcupine

He spent his days
    Roaming
Here and about
    Searching,
    Looking,
Never finding
    a place
To truly fit.

Failure

I am scattered
As chaff
And change
Like the chameleon
To blend
Amongst the rock
And ash.

Paranoia

The friendly smile
Becomes
The accusing grin.
The clear blue
Eyes
Become as glass.

The once love
Becomes a grip
So tight
You cannot
Breathe.

Fear

Your scars
Frighten me
At times.

I do not
Know much
About porcupines
Except
For their
Quills.

I do not
Know much
About love
Except
It hurts
Sometimes.

Phillip

My dear, dear
Phillip
You need not
A Purple Heart
For bravery in
War.

You have
Indeed
Fought a battle
Most could not.

Your reward?
The courage
You give away.

In Contrast

The stars at night
When there are no clouds
Are more magnificent
Than the sun.
However, it is the sun
That makes the lily bloom.

Rats

Tomorrow seems
    a maze.
Yesterday
    a myth.
Today?
    a mirage.

Combat

He was placed
In a hard
Plaster mold
While yet young.

But the mold
Cracked
Irreparably
When he smiled.

The General

He limps through
My dreams
And I am restless
To heal
His wounds
And smooth
His hurt.

Roads

My path leads
Into tomorrow
Beneath
The shadows
Of my peers.

They stand
As tall oaks
Sometimes
Blocking the sun.

Contentment

The donkey
Walked slowly
And dreamed
Of being
A unicorn.

Musing

The Cheshire sat
Curled quietly
By the crackling fire
And smiled a
Cheshire smile
While the tabby
And calico
Played
With string.

Changes

As we change
Costumes
And masks
We sometimes fail
To see
That those we love
Are no longer
Part
Of our play.

Music

Why is it
That the music
We heard
Yesterday
Makes us dance
A different
Step today?

Perhaps
It is because
We dance
To the beat
Of the heart.

Self-Esteem

Mirrors are meant
For gazing into,
Not for shattering
The reflections
We see in them.

Beginnings

The monkey fell
From his shoulders
And he followed
The Light.
Now, please hold
My hand
As I show you
Feelings
Not made of plastic.

Seasons

Sunflowers
In winter ice.
Bright reminders
Of hope.

Prism

My mind seems
As a prism
Reflecting life's events.

Unlike the prism
I reflect inward
Twisting reality
Until the light
Burns my soul.

Lilacs

Long after you, Dad,
Followed the lilacs.
Growing to the top of
My sill.
Deep purple.

With the lilacs
Came the
Honeysuckle
And the hummingbirds,
The long summers.

Lilacs still grow
In the fields
And their scent
Overwhelms me.

Chills

If I were brave
I would smile
When you frown

And laugh
When you cry.

Instead,
I feel
A chill.

Away

You're going away
"Not for long"
But "away."

Maybe I'll
Visit my mother
Or clean a closet,
Or maybe
I'll just sit.

You've gone before
And I've survived,
But, this time,
I'm not so sure.

What if I meet
Someone who is less than
Kind?

What if
It rains all week?

What if
I don't
Miss you?

Gardens

You gave me the sunshine
To put in my pocket
And a few clouds
To break the days.
Now I'm full grown
And give to you
All my love
And all my tomorrows.

Rainy Days

When I heard you crying
I was at a loss for words
I had been bathed in your laughter
For so long.
I tried a little humor,
A little distraction,
But still the tears flowed.

Oh, if I could only hold
You in my arms
And absorb all the tears
And show you the sunshine.

But the clouds
Hang over me as well.

Win or Lose?

As I search my mind
And try to remember
Our most loving time,

I pass by the time
Our eyes met and laughed
Or the time
You held me
For an hour.

I seem to remember
The time you squeezed
My hand
When I was the loser.

When I'm Angry

When I'm angry
At you
I cry.

I cry
Because
At that moment
You are less than perfect,
Less than kind.

I cry
Because
I cannot say
I like you
At that moment.

I cry
Because
I cannot say
I like me
At that moment.

Balances

Enough self-love
A few smiles
Plenty of sunshine
A little rain
And a cool soul,
I am content.

Statistics

Are gains and losses
Measured
In columns?

Is self-esteem
Measured
By pros and cons?

Is love
Measured
By commitment
Or time?

Comparison

Comparison
Of oneself
To another
Is often
Bitter.

Why is it
We see
Only others'
Beauty
And only our
Supposed flaws?

Why must
We be placed
On a scale
With another?

After all,
Don't we all
Have our own
weight?

Visions

White gliding seabird
Glistening wings of satin
With freedom as wind.

Shadows

At times we
       see through
Chantily veils
With just a
       glimpse of
       the future.

The veil was
       never meant
       to be lifted
For,
       it is the
       veil
That keeps us
       searching
       for the Light